THE I

RECIPES

BOOK

DR. RITA BROOKS

COPYRIGHT

Table of Contents

CHAPTER 1

Introduction

The ancient Indian name for rice-"Dhanya," meaning "sustenance for the human race" — indicates the crop's age-old importance. Man has cultivated rice since prehistoric times. Specimens of rice discovered in China date back to 5000 BC.

Rice as a cultivated crop in Asia originated in tropical India. All Hindu scriptures mention rice and all offerings to God include rice, an indication of the antiquity of the crop.

Rice was introduced into Indonesia by

Deutero-Malayans that immigrated to

this region about 1599 BC. Indonesia is

the land where a race of rice called

javanica originated. In fact, the name

Java is said to mean "island of rice."

Japan has long been famous for the

excellence of its rice and rice cultivation

methods. Rice has also been grown in Sri

Lanka (formerly Ceylon) since time

immemorial. Much later, rice cultivation

spread farther west. The Greeks learned

of rice from the Persians and medieval

Europe got it from the Saracens. The crop was introduced in northern Italy in the 15th century. The Malays brought rice to Madagascar and Indians introduced it in the East African islands. The Moors brought rice to Spain and the Turks introduced it over much of the southeastern part of Europe. The Portuguese introduced rice in Brazil and the Spaniards in Central America and parts of South America. The crop was introduced in Hawaii in 1853. The French

Rice came to Japan by way of China. brought it to New Caledonia and the Germans to New Guinea.

Rice cultivation in the United States of

America dates back to about 1646 AD.

The cereal was introduced in Virginia but

was first cultivated in South Carolina.

Presently, rice is cultivated on a

commercial scale in California, Arkansas,

Louisiana, Mississippi, Texas, and South

Carolina.

Rice has been grown commercially in

Australia since 1924. The North Island of

New Zealand also grows rice

successfully.

Rice grows from 55 °N latitude to

37.5 °S, from an altitude of 3,000 m in the Himalayas to places below sea level. It grows on slopes of mountain ranges to areas with 2 meters deep standing water.

Thus, rice is the most versatile food crop cultivated in the modern world.

Food Value

About 85% of the rice kernel is carbohydrates, most of which are in the endosperm. Freshly harvested rice contains 72-75% starch. The protein content of milled rice is low (8-9%), but its digestibility is high, being 96.5 for the

whole grain and 98% for milled rice. The
fat content of rice is low (2-2.4%); about
85% is removed in the process of
milling.

The amount of fat-soluble Vitamins A and
D in rice is negligible, but the Vitamin E
content is considerable. Husked rice has
a high Vitamin B content, at least one-
tenth that of dried yeast. The riboflavin
content is low and Vitamin C is
practically absent.

Rice loses considerable nutrients through
milling and polishing.

Before cooking, it is customary to wash rice, often with several changes of water, to remove dust, insects, husk, and other impurities. Washing dissolves some of the nutrients from the grain, the amount removed depending on the degree of milling and the amount of washing.

Methods of Cooking

Methods of cooking rice vary in different countries. Habitual rice-eaters say there is no one way to cook rice; some varieties of rice and rice grown in certain localities require different treatments.

There are four main methods of cooking rice (FAD 1948) 1 :

1. Large amounts of water are used and he excess is drained away, carrying with it much starch that has been rendered soluble.

2. Rinsed raw rice is immersed in water, just enough to swell the grains properly, and cooked in a double boiler or over a slow fire—to avoid charring at the bottom—until the water is fully absorbed. Ensure the complete removal of the films

of soluble starch on the surface of the grain's.

Boiling, after which the water is drained off and the rice is steamed to a state of tenderness in a pan or basket in an enclosed space over freely boiling water.

3. The cooked rice is often rinsed to ensure the complete removal of the films of soluble starch on the surface of the grain's.

4. Rice is sometimes half-cooked by butter before it is cooked for any kind of dish.

Rice is always eaten with vegetables, pulses, meat, fish, or seafood. A variety of dishes around the world are made with rice

CHAPTER 2

RECIPES

"21" Club Rice Pudding

- 1 qt Milk

- 1 pt Heavy cream

- 1/2 t Salt

- 1 Vanilla bean

- 3/4 c Long-grained rice

- 1 c Granulated sugar

- 1 Egg yolk

- 1 1/2 c Whipped cream

Raisins (optional)

Direction

In a heavy saucepan, combine the milk, cream, salt, vanilla bean and 4 cup of the sugar and bring to a boil. Stirring well, add the rice.

Allow the mixture to simmer gently, covered, for 1 3/4 hours over a very low flame, until rice is soft. Remove from the heat and cool slightly. Remove the vanilla bean. Blending well, stir in the remaining 1/4 cup of sugar and the egg yolk. Allow to cool a bit more. Preheat the broiler. Stir in all but 2 tablespoons of the whipped cream; pour the mixture into individual crocks or a souffle dish. (Raisins my be placed in the bottom of the dishes, if desired.) After spreading the remaining whipped cream in a thin layer over the top, place the crocks or dish under the broiler until the pudding is lightly browned. Chill before serving.

15-Minute Chicken & Rice Dinner

1 T vegetable oil

4 (4-6-oz.) fresh boneless, skinless

chicken breasts

1 10.75-oz. can cream of chicken soup

1 1/3 c water or 2% milk

21

1 1/2 c quick-cooking rice, uncooked

Direction

Heat oil in a large nonstick skillet over medium-high heat. Add chicken; cover. Cook 4 minutes on each side or until cooked thoroughly.

Remove chicken from skillet. Add soup and water; stir to mix and bring to a boil. Stir in rice, then top with chicken; cover. Reduce heat to low and cook 5 minutes.

Comments: Completely cooked in one skillet, this tasty chicken and rice dish is easily and quickly assembled. Add a

salad and crusty bread if desired.

Almond and Rice Flour Bread with Poppy Seeds

1/2 c Whole almonds, with skins

1 1/2 c Brown rice flour

4 t Baking powder

1/4 t Salt

3 t Poppy seeds

1/2 c Plain low-fat yogurt

1/2 c Water

1 lg Whole egg

1 lg Egg white white

2 T Vegetable oil

Direction

Preheat oven to 350F. Butter an 8 x
4inch loaf pan.

Place almonds and 1/2 cup of the flour
in bowl of a food processor and grind
until a fine meal is formed++the flour
will prevent the nuts from turning oily.

Add remaining rice flour, the baking

powder, salt and 2 teaspoons of the

poppy seeds; process briefly.

Combine yogurt, water, whole egg, egg

white and oil in a 2-cup measuring cup.

With processor motor running, pour

liquid ingredients through feed tube

over flour mixture, processing just long

enough to mix.

Transfer batter to prepared pan.

Sprinkle with remaining poppy seeds,

and bake for 55 minutes. Turn out onto a rack to cool. (Bread slices best after several hours, or the next day).

Makes one 18-ounce loaf (18 slices).

PER SLICE: 90 calories, 3 g protein, 11 g carbohydrate, 4 g fat (1 g saturated), 12 mg cholesterol, 115 mg sodium, 1 g fiber.

Almond Tuna and Rice

1 cn VEG-ALL Mixed

- Vegetables (16 oz)

1 c Mayonnaise

1 cn Tuna (12.5 oz)

2 c Cooked rice

1/2 c Chopped green pepper

2 t Dill weed

1 c Fresh bread crumbs

1/2 c Slivered almonds

Drain VEG-ALL; combine liquid with mayonnaise, blending until smooth.

Stir in tuna, rice, green pepper, dill and vegetables.

Spoon into greased 2-quart casserole dish.

In small skillet, melt butter; stir in bread crumbs and almonds, coat well and spoon over mixture in casserole.

Bake at 375'F. for 30 minutes or until bubbly and lightly browned.

Antipasto Rice

1 1/2 c Water

1/2 c Tomato juice

1 c Uncooked rice

1 t Dried basil leaves

1 t Dried oregano leaves

1/2 t Salt; optional

1 cn Artichoke hearts;

- drained & quartered (14 oz.)

1 Jars Roasted red peppers;

- dr d and chopped (7 oz.)

1 cn Sliced ripe olives (2-1/4 oz.)

2 T Fresh parsley; snipped

2 T Lemon juice

1/2 t Ground black pepper

2 T Parmesan; grated

Direction

Basil, oregano and salt in saucepan. Heat
to boiling; stir once or twice. Lower heat
to simmer; cover with a tight-fitting lid.
Cook for 15 to 20 minutes. Stir in
artichokes, red peppers, olives, parsley,

lemon juice and black pepper. Cook an
additional 5 minutes or until thoroughly
heated. Sprinkle with cheese

Apricot and Rice Muffins

1 1/2 c Flour

2/3 c Whole Wheat Flour

1/3 c Rice Bran

1 T Baking powder

1 t Cinnamon

1 c Cooked, brown Rice

1 1/2 c Dried Apricots, diced

1/2 c Raisins

1/2 c Dried Prunes

1/4 c Walnuts, chopped

1 c No Fat Yogurth

2/3 c Maple Syrup

1/4 c Oil

1/4 c Eggsubstitute or

1 Egg, lightly beaten

Direction

In large bowl combine flours, rice bran, baking powder and cinnamon.

Stir in rice, apricots, raisins, prunes and walnuts.

In a small bowl, whisk together the yogurth, syrup, oil and egg.

Pour over dry ingridients and fold together until just moistened. Do not overmix.

Line 18 muffin cups with paper liners. Divide the batter amoung cups.

Bake at 350 F until edges and tops begin

to brown, about 45 minutes.

Armenian Rice Pilaf

- 1/4 lb Butter or margarine

- 1/2 c Vermicelli

- 2 c Uncooked long-grain rice

- 4 c Boiling hot chicken broth

- 1 t MSG (optional)

- Salt

Direction

Melt butter in heavy pan or Dutch oven. Break vermicelli in small pieces, add to pan and cook until golden brown, stirring constantly.

Add rice and stir until rice is well coated with butter. Add boiling broth and MSG and season to taste with salt. Cook, covered, over low heat until liquid is absorbed, about 25 minutes. Stir lightly with fork. Let stand in warm place 15 to 20 minutes before serving.

Aromatic Chicken with Rice (Malaysia)

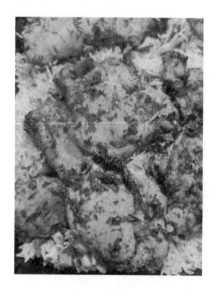

3 c Cooked rice

1 Chicken (3 pounds)

1 Onion

3 T Sesame oil

2 T Light soy sauce

1/2 t Salt

1/4 t Pepper

Direction

Spread cooked rice in a pie pan. Chop
chicken into large pieces. Cut onion into
wedges. In a wok or large pan heat
sesame oil and brown the chicken with
the onions until the onions are
transparent. Add soy sauce and sprinkle
with salt and pepper. Put the chicken on
the cooked rice in the pie plate. Steam

for about 30 minutes or until the chicken is done. Serve warm.

If you have a rice cooker, you can just put the braised onions and chicken on top of the raw rice and cook it that way.

Arroz Amarillo con Camarones - Yellow Rice & Shrimp Casser

1/2 c Olive oil

1 sm Onion; chopped

1 sm Green pepper; chopped

1 Garlic clove; minced

1 Parsley sprig

1 lg Ripe tomato peeled, seeded & chopped

1 Bay leaf

1/4 t Nutmeg

1/4 t Cumin

1/4 t Thyme

1 pn Saffron; toasted

1 lb Shrimp, raw shelled, deveined

1 c -Hot water

1/4 c Dry white wine

1 T Lemon juice

1 T Salt

1/2 t Hot sauce

2 c Long grain white rice

2 1/2 c -Water

1/2 c Beer

Cooked peas

Pimiento strips

Parsley bouquets

Direction

Use a 3-quart casserole with lid. An
earthenware casserole is preferable,
specially if you wish to add a touch of
Spain to a dinner party. However, I know
that good earthenware is hard to find
today. I have 2 casseroles that I've had
for 15 years.

Heat oil in casserole. Saute onion and
pepper until transparent. Add garlic,

parsley, tomato, bay leaf, nutmeg, cumin and thyme. Mix well, cover, and cook over low heat until mushy (about 15 minutes). The saffron should be toasting on the lid in the little brown paper.

Add the shrimp to the saute and cook until it turns pink. Dissolve the saffron in the 1 cup hot water. Combine with wine, lemon juice, salt and hot sauce. Pour into casserole, stir to mix, and cook covered minutes more. Now add the rice and the 2 1/2 cups of water.

Distribute ingredients well in casserole. Bring to a quick boil, STIR ONCE, and place in preheated 325 degree F. oven

for only minutes.

Remove from oven, uncover, and garnish

with peas, pimientos, and parsley. Pour

beer over all. Cover again and allow to

stand 15 minutes longer, before serving.

Arroz Con Pollo (mexican Stewed Chicken With Rice)

3 lb Chicken, cut into pieces

1/4 c Cooking oil

1/2 c Chopped onion

1 Clove garlic, sliced

- paper thin

1/2 c Chopped green pepper

1 cn Tomatoes

1/2 t Sait

1/4 t Pepper

1/2 t Paprika

4 Cloves

2 sm Bay leaves

1 c Raw rice

1 1 O ounce package frozen peas,

1 Sweet red pepper

~cut into 1/4" pieces

Direction

Dry the pieces of chicken with paper
toweling. Place the oil in a large skiilet
and saute the chicken until golden
brown. Add the onion, garlic and green

pepper and saute until tbe onion is transparent and glazed.

Then add the tomatoes, salt, pepper, paprika, cloves and bay leaves.

Bring to a rollng boil, and then turn thc heat back to simmer. Cover and simmer for 25 minutes. Add the rice; stir it in well. Cover and simmer for 20 minutes longer, or until the grains of rice are tender.

Sprinkle the peas and pepper over the top, and cook, uncovered, for 5 minutes more. Serves 6. If you wish, remove the cloves and bay leaves before serving.

Arroz Dulce (sweet Rice)

Yield: 10 Servings

1 c Rice

1/2 c Raisins

1 1/2 Cinnamon sticks

1 c Sugar

1 T Grated gingerroot

1 c Canned coconut cream

2 c Milk

1/2 t Vanilla

1/4 c Unsalted butter

Ground cinnamon

Direction

Soak rice and raisins in water to cover 1/2 hour. Bring 2 cups water to boil in large saucepan. Drain rice and raisins and add to boiling water with cinnamon sticks and 1/4 cup sugar. Cook over low heat until rice is tender. Boil gingerroot in 1/2 cup water 5 minutes, strain and blend liquid with remaining 3/4 cup sugar, coconut cream, milk and vanilla.

Add this mixture with butter to rice. Cover and cook over low heat until milk is absorbed, stirring every 5 to 10 minutes. Spoon into serving dish or individual custard cups, sprinkle with cinnamon and chill.

Arroz Verde (Green Rice)

4 Poblano chilies; or 4 green;peppers, each 4 inches in;diameter

 4 c Chicken stock; fresh or can

 1 c Parsley, fresh; coarsely;chopped

 1/2 c Onion; coarsely chopped

 1/4 t Garlic; finely chopped

 1 t Salt

 1/8 t Black pepper; freshly ground

 1/4 c Olive oil

 2 c Long grain rice; raw

Direction

Roast the chilies or peppers, remove
their skins, stems, seeds and thick white
membranes and discard. Chop the chilies
into chunks.

Combine 1 cup of the chunks and 1/2
cup of stock in the jar of a blender and
blend at high speed for 15 seconds{d
ohen gradually add the remaining chilies
and the parsley, onions, garlic, salt and
pepper, blending until the mixture is
reduced to a smooth puree. (To make
the sauce by hand, puree the chilies,
parsley, onions and garlic, a cup or so at

a time, in a food mill set over a bowl. Discard any pulp left in the mill. Stir in 1/2 cup of stock and the salt and pepper.) Pour the oil into a 2 to 3 quart casserole and set it over moderate heat. When the oil is hot but not smoking, add the rice and stir constantly for 2 to 3 minutes until the grains are coated with oil. Do not let them brown. Now add the pureed chili mixture and simmer, stirring

occasionally, for 5 minutes. Meanwhile, bring the remaining /2 cups of stock to a boil in a small saucepan and pour it over the rice. Return to a boil, cover the casserole and reduce the heat to its lowest point.

Simmer undisturbed for 18 to 20 minutes, or until the rice is tender and has absorbed all the liquid. Before serving, fluff the rice with a fork. If the rice must wait, remove the cover and drape the pan loosely with a towel. Place in a preheated 250 degree (F) oven to keep warm.

Baked Chicken and Rice

1 lb boneless skinless chicken

- breasts

1 can cream of mushroom soup

1 c water

1 envelope onion soup mix

1 c rice, (not instant)

Direction

Place chicken in prepared casserole dish.

In separate bowl mix together remaining ingredients. Pour over chicken.

58

Cover and bake at 375F. for 1 hour.

Basic Cooked Rice - Prudhomme

2 c Uncooked rice

2 1/2 c Basic stock (Prudhomme)

1 1/2 T Onions, chopped very fine

1 1/2 T Celery, chopped very fine

1 1/2 T Bell peppers,chopped vy fine

1 1/2 T Unsalted butter (preferred)

1/2 t Salt

1/8 t Garlic powder

white pepper

black pepper

cayenne pepper

Direction

In a 5x9x2-1/2-inch loaf pan, combine all ingredients; mix well. Seal pan snuggly with aluminum foil. Bake at 350F until rice is tender, about 1 hour, 10 minutes. Serve immediately. However, you can count on the rice staying hot for 45 minutes and warm for 2 hours. To reheat leftover rice, either use a double boiler or warm the rice in a skillet with unsalted butter.

Beef Teriyaki And Rice

3 T Soy sauce

1 T Dry sherry

2 t Brown sugar

1 1/4 t Garlic powder

1 t Ground ginger

3/4 lb Flank steak strips Or

Chicken breasts

1 T Oil

3 c Bite size vegetables

1 c Beef broth

4 t Cornstarch

Water to thin sauce

Necessary

*Three cups of veggies - suggest slant
cut carrots, green onions, green or red
pepper chunks, a few pea pods if you
have them. Mix soy sauce, sherry, brown
sugar and seasonings. Add beef or
chicken. Let stand 10 minutes to
marinate.

Stir fry meat in hot oil in wok until
browned, remove. Add vegetables.

Stir fry until tender crisp. Mix broth and cornstarch, add to wok.

Bring to boil, boil 1 minute. Replace meat to wok to coat.

Serve over rice.

Black Beans and Rice

1 1/2 lb dried black turtle beans

1 large bell pepper, diced

1 hot pepper (optional)

tabasco (optional)

4 onions, diced

6 cloves garlic, chopped

3/4 c celery, diced

1/4 c parsley, chopped

2 T oregano, chopped

2 T basil, chopped

2 bay leaves

ground cloves

1/2 t ground cumin

4 beef boullion cubes

1 lb lean bulk pork sausage

1 lb pork, boneless cubed

1 lb stew beef chunks

1/2 lb ham, smoked (1/2" cubes)

1 1/2 lb smoked link sausage cut

- into 1" to 2" lengths

salt to taste

pepper to taste

2 T vinegar

Direction

Wash and look for gravel then soak overnight in a bowl being sure beans

are well covered with water. For cooking use a large crock pot.

First, brown bulk sausage in a skillet and pour off excess grease. Add other meats and stir to brown. Add bell pepper, onion, garlic, celery, and spices. Salt and pepper moderately, taste after cooking several hours and add more if needed.

Add beans and soak water. If necessary add more water to cover entire ingredients by at least two inches. Stir in four bouillon cubes. Cover and cook on crock pot high for three hours then turn to low for at least six hours.

Serve beans and meat over rice. Serve in a soup bowl and top with fresh chopped onion.

Blackeyed Peas and Rice

1 x Dried black-eyed peas

1 x Lipton Rice 'n' Sauce Cajun

1 x Stew Meat

1 x Bell pepper

1 x Onion

1 T Pepper

1 t Creole or Cajun seasoning

1 x Cayenne pepper or hot sauce

Direction

Look thru peas for rocks and wash

through 3 waters. Soak peas in water

69

overnight in fridge. The next day, throw out water they soaked in; some claim this keeps beans from giving you a problem, but stay on this diet a couple weeks and you won't have a problem anyway. It goes away.

Wash stew meat and put stew meat and pre-soaked peas in big pot on stove and bring to boil, with PLENTY of water. Add seasonings to taste. If you use Cajun seasoning it contains salt; so don't add extra salt!!!! Otherwise, add salt to taste. When stew meat and peas come to a boil, reduce to Medium and keep watching to add water so they don't scorch. After about 40 minutes add packet of Rice and Sauce, preferably Cajun flavor. Start watching the water really carefully now, and add a pint from time to time. After about minutes of rice cooking, add bell pepper, onion, and more seasonings if you need.

(This dish is good hot and peppery) Everything should be ready at the same time. When test bite shows all is ready, eat!

Black-eyed Peas And Rice Salad

3 c Hot cooked (boiled) rice

1 1/2 c Cooked black-eyed peas =OR=-

10 oz -Frozen black-eyed peas (cooked
according to package directions)

1 T Dijon-style mustard

1 t Salt (or to taste)

Freshly ground pepper

3 T Red wine vinegar

3/4 c Extra-virgin olive oil (or

- part safflower oil)

1 md Onion; minced

1 Garlic clove; minced

1 lg Carrot; peeled and grated

1/4 c Minced chives or parsley

1 Head of radicchio =OR=-

- Boston

- lettuce (for garnish)

Direction

COOK THE RICE AND THE PEAS in
advance.

PREPARE THE VINAIGRETTE: WHISK

THE MUSTARD, salt, pepper and vinegar
until dissolved. Dribble in the oil while

whisking. Toss the black-eyed peas and the rice with the vinaigrette until everything is nicely coated. Mix in the onion, garlic, carrot and chives or parsley. Bring to room temperature before serving. This dish can be prepared a day ahead and refrigerated, covered. Place in a bowl and surround with lettuce leaves; serve at room temperature.

Blanched Gai Lan Dressed with Rice Wine and Oyster Sauce

2 T Oyster sauce

2 T Chicken stock

1 T Shao Hsing wine, or

- dry sherry

1/2 t Sugar

1/2 t Sesame oil 1 To 1 1/2 lb gai lan (Chinese broccoli)

1 t Salt

1 T Peanut oil

Direction

Combine the oyster sauce, chicken stock, Shao Hsing wine, sugar and sesame oil in a small saucepan. Bring to a boil and cook until sauce thickens. Set aside.

Wash the gai lan in cold water. Trim off and discard the tough bottoms. Peel stalks if they are thick and tough; leave gai lan whole or cut into thirds.

Bring 3 to 4 quarts of water to a boil in a wok or stock pot; add the salt and oil. Add the greens, bring back to a second boil. Turn off the heat and let greens stand for a minute or two. When the

green stalks brighten, test one for

doneness. It should be tender and crisp.

Drain immediately and shake off excess

water.

Transfer to a platter, pour dressing over,

and serve immediately.

Bombay Rice & Lentils

- 1/2 Onion,medium-size,chopped

- 2 T Salad oil

- 1 c Rice,brown,uncooked

- 1 T Tomato paste

- 2 1/2 c Water

- 1/4 t Cinnamon

- 1/4 c Lentils,uncooked

- 1/2 t Salt,seasoned

- 1/2 c Raisins

- 1/2 c Pinenuts

Saute onion in oil in large skillet until soft.

Add rice; cook, stirring, several minutes.

Combine tomato paste, water, cinnamon and lentils in a bowl; add to rice.

Bring mixture to a boil; cover tightly, reduce heat and simmer 30 minutes.

Stir in seasoned salt, raisins and pinenuts.

Grease an 8-inch-square baking dish; pour in rice mixture.

Cover and bake in preheated 350'F. oven 20 to 30 minutes.

Brazilian Chicken Rice Soup

- 1 3 lb Chicken
- 1 Bay leaf
- 1 Medium onion, quartered
- 1 Whole clove
- 2 Ripe tomatoes, quartered
- 1 Carrot, cut into 1" pieces
- 1/4 c Chopped celery leaves
- 20 Black peppercorns, tied in
- A piece of cheesecloth
- 1/2 c Uncooked white rice
- Salt & freshly ground black
- Pepper
- 3 Carrots, thinly sliced on
- The diagonal

- 1/4 c Finely chopped flat-leaf
- Parsley

Direction

Wash the chicken thoroughly. Remove the skin and any pieces of fat.

Pin the bay leaf to 1 onion quarter with the clove. Place the chicken in a large pot with the tomatoes, onion quarters, 1 carrot, celery leaves, and peppercorn bundle. Add 10 cups cold water and bring to a boil. Using a ladle, skim off the fat and foam that rise to the surface. Reduce the heat and simmer for 1 hour, skimming often to remove the fat.

Remove the chicken from the broth and let cool. Strain the broth into a large saucepan, pressing the vegetables to extract the juices. (There should be about 8 cups of broth.) Pull the chicken meat off the bones and shred or finely dice it.

Add the rice, salt, and pepper to the broth and simmer for 10 minutes.

Add the thinly sliced carrots and celery to the soup with the shredded chicken and half the parsley. Simmer the soup for another 10 minutes, or until the rice is tender. Correct the seasoning, adding

salt and pepper to taste. Sprinkle with
the remaining parsley and serve at
once.

Brown Rice & Wheat Berries (Vegan)

- 2 1/4 c Water
- 1/3 c Wheat berries
- 1/3 c Brown rice
- 1 T Saute fluid (pick your a
- Compatible favoriet)
- 1/4 c Chopped scallion
- 1/4 t Salt
- 1/8 t Pepper

Direction

In 2qt pan, boil water. Add berries, return to boil. Reduce heat, simmer, covered, 1 hour. Stir in brown rice.

Cover, simmer 50 minutes longer. 5 minutes before rice is finished, saute scallion until softened. Combi ne with rice and wheat mixture, along with spices.

Brown Rice Casserole

- 4 c Cooked brown rice
- Half block of tofu
- 1 lg Onion
- 2 md Carrots
- 2 Celery stalks
- 1 Green pepper
- 2 md Zucchini =OR=-
    - other summer squash
- 6 oz Mushrooms, wiped clean
- 1 T Olive oil
- 1 T Butter
- 3 Garlic cloves finely chopped
- 1 t Nutritional yeast (optional)
- 1 t Ground cumin seeds

- 1 t Salt

- 1 c Mushroom broth; -=OR=-

    - Vegetable stock, or water

- 6 oz Grated cheese (Jack,

    - muenster, Cheddar or

      Gouda)

- Pepper

- Fresh herbs, for garnish

    - (Parsley

    - or Cilantro, Thyme,

    - Marjoram)

Direction

COOK RICE. SET THE TOFU on a slanted

board or pan to drain, and prepare the

vegetables. Chop the onion, carrots, celery, pepper, and zucchini into pieces about 1/2-inch square. Quarter mushrooms if they are small, and cut them into sixths or eighths if they are large. Cut the tofu into 1/2-inch cubes. Heat the olive oil and the butter and fry the onion over medium heat until it is lightly browned, about 5 minutes.

Add the garlic, nutritional yeast, if using, cumin and salt. Stir until blended and cook for 1 minute. Add the carrots, celery, green pepper and 1/2 cup of the liquid, cover pan, and braise the vegetables until they begin to soften, about 5 minutes. Add the zucchini and mushrooms and cook 7 to 10 minutes. The vegetables should be nearly, but not completely, cooked. If the pan gets dry while they cook, add a little more liquid. Preheat oven to 350F. Combine the vegetables with rice and cheese. Season with salt and plenty of freshly ground black pepper.

Gently mix in the tofu, and put mixture into lightly oiled casserole.

Add a little more liquid to moisten. Cover with foil and bake 1/2 hour.

Remove foil and bake 15 minutes.

Garnish with fresh herbs.

Brown Rice Jambalaya

- 1/2 lb Diced ham or bacon (cut bacon crosswise into thin strips)
- 4 Chicken legs (2 1/2 pounds)
- 1 lb Cajun-style sausage
- 3 md Garlic cloves, peeled
- 1 md Onion, peeled, cubed
- 1 md Green bell pepper, cored, cut in 1 inch squares
- 2 md Tomatoes, peeled, cored, quartered
- 1 1/2 c Raw brown rice
- 1/2 t Each, dried oregano leaves, dried thyme leaves, file
- Powder, ground black pepper

91

- 1/4 t Each, cayenne pepper, ground cumin

- 3 c Chicken broth

- Salt

- 1/2 lb Peeled, deveined raw shrimp

Direction

Put ham or bacon in a 4-quart soup kettle and cook over low heat until

fat is rendered. Increase heat to medium and stir until cooked, about 5 minutes.

Remove chicken skin, cut meat off the bones and then cut boneless chicken into bite-size pieces. Add to kettle or skillet with bacon or ham and toss until color turns pale, about 4 minutes. Remove bacon or ham and chicken with a slotted spoon and put on paper toweling; set

 aside. Add sausage to kettle and brown all over, about to 8 minutes; remove. Leave 2 tablespoons fat in kettle; pour off and discard remaining fat.

 Insert metal blade in food processor. Mince garlic by adding to machine with motor on. Add onion and chop very coarsely with half second pulses. Add green pepper and process with half-second pulses until mixture is chopped to medium consistency. Add mixture to kettle and stir over low heat until softened, about 10 minutes. Process tomatoes until pureed; set aside.

Add rice to ingredients in kettle and stir over low heat for 2 minutes.

Then stir in oregano Thyme, file, black pepper, cayenne pepper and cumin. Add tomatoes and broth. Stir well and let mixture to boiling.

Reduce heat to low, cover and cook rice mixture 15 to 20 minutes. Cut sausage into 1/4-inch thick coin like slices. Mix sausage, ham and chicken pieces into rice. Cover and cook until rice is tender (rice may not absorb all the liquid) about 20 minutes longer. Taste and adjust seasoning, adding salt as needed. Stir shrimp into hot rice mixture, cover pot and let stand for 8 to 10 minutes. Serve rice with shrimp, meats and liquid.

Brown Rice Pilaf

- 1/2 t Instant chicken bouillon

- 1 c Sliced fresh Mushrooms

- 3/4 c Brown Rice, quick cooking

- 1/2 c Shredded Carrot

- 1/4 t Dried Marjoram, crushed

- 1/4 c Thinly sliced Green Onion

- 2 T Snipped fresh Parsley

Direction

In a medium saucepan stir together bouillon granules and 1 cup water.

Bring to boiling. Stir in mushrooms, brown rice, carrot, marjoram, and dash pepper. Reduce heat and simmer,

96

covered, for 12 minutes. Remove from heat; let stand for 5 minutes. Add green onion and parsley; toss lightly with a fork. Serve immediately.

Brussels Sprout and Rice

- 1 cn 10 3/4 ounces condensed

- Cream of Mushroom soup

- 1 c Milk

- 1 T Butter

- 1 t Salt

- 3/4 t Caraway Seed

- 2/3 c Regular Rice

- 2 package Frozen Brussel Sprouts

- 10 oz each, cut in half

Direction

About 40 minutes before serving: In 12

inch skillet, over medium heat, heat

undiluted soup, milk, 1 cup water,

butter, salt and caraway seed to boiling;

stirring occasionally. Stir in rice; reduce

heat to low; cover and simmer 15

minutes. Stir in brussel sprouts; cover

and continue to cook 15 minutes or until

rice and brussel sprouts are tender;

stirring occasionally.

Buttered Saffron Rice

- 2 t Saffron;leaf saffron
- 2 T Milk; warm
- 1 T -Salt
- 2 c Rice, basmati
- 4 T Butter

Direction

Place saffron in small, dry, hot pan over medium heat about 1 minute or just until fragrant. Crumble into milk. Fill large pot with about 13 cups water; add salt and bring to boil. Meanwhile, place rice in medium bowl and cover with cold water. Immediately drain rice through colander. Wash and drain two more times. When water is boils, add rice

and stir once; bring to boil. Cook 5 minutes; rice should be slightly hard in the centre. Drain in colander and place in ovenproof dish.

Drizzle saffron milk over rice, tossing over a couple of times very gently. Divide butter into four pieces; place over rice. Cut pieces of aluminium foil 2 inches larger than rim of dish; place on top of dish; place lid on foil. Bake in preheated 300F oven to 50 minutes, checking after 40 minutes to see if rice is

cooked. Serve saffron-coloured

streaked rice spooned on warmed

platter.

Cajun Jambalaya Rice

- 1 md Onion - chopped
- 3 Garlic cloves - finely
- Chopped
- 1 lg Bell pepper - green, cut
- Into 1/2" pieces
- 2 1/2 c Basic chicken stock
- 5 Scallions - finely sliced
- 1 c Brown rice - long grained
- 3 Italian plum tomatoes - Cored, seeded, chopped
- 1/4 lb Turkey ham - baked, all fat
- Removed, 1/2" cubes
- 1/4 t White pepper
- 1/4 t Black pepper - fresh ground

- 3/4 t Cayenne pepper

- 1/2 t Cumin

- 1/4 t Allspice

- 1/4 lb Shrimp - peeked and deveined

- ds Tabasco sauce - (optional)

- 1/4 c Parsley - fresh, chopped

Direction

In an 8-quart pot saute the onion, garlic, and green pepper in 3 Tbsp.

of stock for 5 minutes.

Add two-thirds of the scallions, the rice, and tomatoes, and cook for 5 minutes over medium-low heat, adding a little more of the stock if necessary.

Add the cubed turkey ham, the three peppers, cumin, allspice, and the remaining stock, and cook on very low heat, covered for 40 minutes. Add the shrimp and cook for 2 minutes.

Taste for spiciness. You can add 5-6 drops of Tabasco sauce (I prefer Louisiana Gold Sauce) for a more pungent flavor.

Serve garnished with parsley and the remaining scallions.

Cajun Rice 'N' Sausage

- 3/4 t Paprika

- 1/4 t Anise Seed; lightly crushed

- 1 t Fresh Marjoram; minced

- 2 T Fresh Basil; minced

- 2 ds Tabasco Sauce

- 1/2 t Pickled Jalapeno Peppers -

  minced

- 1 T Worcestershire Sauce

- 1/2 c Canned Tomato Puree

- 14 1/2 oz Can Cut Tomatoes; with

  their juices

- 1/4 lb Chicken Sausage

- 4 c Cooked Brown Rice

- 2 c Stir-Fried Vegetables

- 1/4 lb Cooked Shrimp

- 1 Green Onion; minced

- 1/4 c Parsley; chopped

Direction

Combine paprika, anise seed, marjoram, basil, Tabasco, jalapeno, Worcestershire, tomato puree and canned tomatoes with juice. Stir to combine. Preheat oven to 375?F. Lightly prick sausages with the tines of a fork. Place in a small baking pan and roast for 15 minutes. Remove

from oven; reduce oven temperature to 350?F. Cut sausages into /4" rounds.

Combine rice, sausages, and 1 cup tomato mixture in a 2 quart casserole; par to an even layer. Combine vegetables and shrimp with remaining tomato mixture; spoon over rice and sausages. Cover and bake for 15 minutes, until hot. Stir in green onions and parsley.

Cajun Spiced Chicken and Rice

- 1 T Flour
- 1 Cooking bag
- 1 c Rice, instant
- 1 Bell pepper, cut in chunks
- 1/2 c Onion, chopped
- 1/4 c Celery, sliced
- 1/2 t Thyme leaves
- 1/4 t Salt
- 14 1/2 oz Tomatoes, canned, cut in
- Half
- 1/4 c Water
- 4 To 6 pieces chicken
- 1/4 t Cayenne
- 1/4 t Garlic powder

109

Direction

Preheat oven to 350. Shake flour in cooking bag; place in 13x9x2-inch

baking pan. Combine rice, green pepper, onion, celery, thyme and salt in bag. Add tomatoes and water; squeeze bag to blend ingredients.

Arrange ingredients in an even layer. Combine cayenne pepper and garlic powder; sprinkle lightly over chicken. Place chicken in bag on top of rice mixture. Close bag with nylon tie; make half-inch slits in top. Bake 1 hour or until tender.

Camp Tuna and Rice

- 2 cn Tuna; and liquid

- 1 c Quick-cooking brown rice

- 2 T Instant dried onikon

- 2 T Green pepper flakes

- 1 3/4 c Boiling water

Direction

Heat tuna in its oil in a skillet. Add remaining ingredients and bring to a boil. Cover and cook 15 to 20 minutes.

Carrot-Rice Puree

- 2 T Brown rice, uncooked
- 6 Carrots, scrubbed and chopped in small pieces
- 1 1/3 c Water
- 1 teaspoon sweet butter (optional)

Direction

Place rice and carrots in a saucepan with the water and cover. Simmer until the water is absorbed--about 30 to 40 minutes. When cool enough to handle, puree in blender or food processor with butter until smooth Refrigerate, or freeze leftovers in ice cube tray.

Carrot-Rice Soup

- 1 lb Carrots, peeled and chopped

- 1 md Onion, chopped

- 1 T Margarine

- 4 c Chicken broth, divided

- 1/4 t Dried tarragon leaves

- 1/4 t Ground white pepper

- 2 1/4 c Cooked rice

- 1/4 c Light sour cream

Snipped parsley or mint for garnish

Cook carrots and onion in margarine in large saucepan or Dutch oven over medium-high heat 2-3 minutes or until onion is tender. Add 2 cups broth,

113

tarragon, and pepper. Reduce heat; simmer 10 minutes. Combine vegetables and broth in food processor or blender; process until smooth. Return to saucepan. Add remaining 2 cups broth and rice; thoroughly heat. Dollop soup cream on each serving of soup. Garnish

with parsley.

Catalan Rice

- 2 1/2 c Fish Stock
- 1/4 t Saffron Threads
- 1/4 c Dry White Wine
- 6 T Lard
- 1/2 lb Chorizo, Sliced 1/4"
- 1 1/2 lb Pork Loin, 1" Cubes
- 1 Onion, Thinly Sliced
- 2 Bell Peppers, Julienned
- 2 Tomatoes, Peeled, Seeded
- 3 Large Squid
- 2 c Long-Grained Rice
- 3/4 c Blanched Almonds
- 1/3 c Pine Nuts
- 3 Garlic Cloves, Minced

- 1 c Artichoke Hearts, Drained

- 18 Clams Or Mussels, Scrubbed

- 1/2 c Peas

- 1/4 c Pimientos, Julienned

- 2 T Fresh Parsley, Minced

Direction

Clean squid and cut body sacs into rings. Cut tentacles in half. In a small saucepan, bring stock to a bare simmer. Crush saffron and combine it with wine in a small bowl. In a flameproof casserole or paella pan, heat the lard over moderately high heat. Saute the chorizo and pork, turning them until they are browned. Add the onion, bell peppers, tomatoes, and squid and cook the mixture over moderate heat, stirring, for 15 minutes. Stir in the rice and cook for 1 minute, stirring. Stir in almonds, pine nuts, garlic, saffron mixture, and artichoke hearts. Ladle in enough stock to just cover the rice mixture.

Bring to a boil and simmer it, covered, for 20 minutes. Arrange the clams in the rice, add the peas, and simmer for -15 minutes, or until the rice is just tender and the clams open. Discard any clams that do not open. Garnish with pimientos

and parsley.

Cauliflower & Wild Rice Soup

- 1 md Onion, chopped

- 1 c Thinly sliced celery

- 1 c Sliced fresh mushrooms

- 1/2 c Butter or margarine

- 1/2 c Flour

- 1 qt Chicken broth

- 2 c Cooked wild rice

- 2 c Cauliflower florets, cooked

- 1 c Light cream

Direction

In a large saucepan, saute onion, celery

and mushrooms in butter until tender.

119

Sprinkle with flour. Stir to coat well.

Gradually add chicken broth. Cook and

stir until thickned. Stir in wild rice,

cauliflower and cream until well blended.

Cook gently until heated through. Do not

boil.

Char Kway Teow (Stir-Fried Rice Noodles)

- 2 Chinese sausages (lop cheong)
- 1/4 lb Medium shrimp (36 to 40 per pound), shelled and deveined
- 1 t Salt
- 1/4 lb Cleaned squid, with tentacles
- 1/4 lb Chinese barbecued pork
- 1/4 t White pepper
- 1 1/2 T Dark soy sauce
- 1 1/2 T Light soy sauce
- 1 T Oyster sauce
- 2 lb Fresh rice noodles, in 5/8-inch-wide strips

- 4 T Peanut oil

- 4 Cloves garlic, chopped

- 4 Shallots, sliced (1/2 cup sliced)

- 6 Fresh red chiles, seeded and
  chopped

- 1 c Bean sprouts, tails removed

- 1 c Shredded Chinese cabbage

- 2 lg Eggs

- 4 Green onions, chopped

- Fresh coriander sprigs, for garnish

Direction

Steam the sausages for 10 minutes. Cut
them in thin diagonal slices.

Toss the shrimp with 1/2 teaspoon of the salt. Let them stand for 10 minutes, rinse well with cold water, drain, and pat dry. Cut the squid into 1/4 inch rings and tentacles. Cut the barbecued pork into

1/4-inch-thick slices. Combine the white pepper, soy sauces, and oyster sauce in a bowl; set aside. Just before cooking, put the noodles in a large bowl and pour boiling water over them. Stir gently with

chopsticks to separate the strands, drain, and shake off the excess water. Preheat a wok; when hot, add 2 tablespoons of the oil. Add the remaining

1/2 teaspoon salt and the garlic, shallots, and chiles and cook over medium-high heat until the garlic is golden brown. Increase the heat to high and toss in the shrimp and squid; stirfry until the shrimp turn bright orange and the squid looks opaque white, about 2 minutes. Add the sausage slices, barbecued pork, bean sprouts, and cabbage; toss and stir until the vegetables begin to wilt. Remove everything in the wok to a platter and set aside. Add the remaining 2 tablespoons of oil to the wok; when hot, toss in the well-drained noodles. Gently toss and flip the noodles to heat them through. Be careful not to break them; it is okay if they brown slightly. Push the oodles up the sides of the wok to make a well in the middle; pour in the soy sauce mixture, then toss the noodles gently to sauce them evenly. Make a well again and break the eggs into the middle. Without mixing them with the noodles, scramble the eggs lightly. When the eggs begin to set, add the green onions and return the seafood mixture.

Gently toss together to reheat and mix. Serve hot, with a hot chill sauce for seasoning to taste. Garnish with coriander sprigs.

NOTE:

Both here and in Asia, fresh rice noodles are usually purchased rather than made at home. Look for them in Asian markets or Chinese take-out dim sum shops. This dish can be prepared with dried rice noodles; however, it is worth taking the time to seek out the fresh variety.

Make certain that your wok is well seasoned or the fragile rice noodles will break apart and stick to the pan. Although I hesitate recommending that you cook with a non stick wok or skillet, they will work fine if you are more

comfortable with them.

Cheese and Rice Casserole

- 2 1/2 c Brown rice, cooked

- 3 Green onions, chopped

- 1 c Low fat cottage cheese

- 1 t Dried dill

- 1/4 c Grated parmesan cheese

- 1/2 c 1% milk

Direction

Combine all in a mixing bowl. Pour into

casserole dish sprayed with

nonstick spray.

Bake at 350F for 15-20 minutes.

Chestnuts With Rice

- 1 md Onion, sliced finely

- 1/4 lb Mushrooms, sliced

- Margarine as required

- 1 t All-purpose flour

- 1/2 c Stock

- 1 lb Chestnuts, boiled

- Salt & black pepper

- 1/2 c White wine

- 2 c Cooked rice

Direction

Saute onion & mushrooms in margarine till brown. Add flour & blend.

Gradually add stock. Stir till smooth.

Add peeled & chopped chestnuts

& mix well. Season. Add white wine,

heat to boiling point & serve over rice.

Chicken & Rice

- 2 lg Chicken breasts [boneless skin on or off]
- 1 cn Cream of chicken soup
- 1 cn Cream of celery soup
- 1 cn Cream of mushroom soup
- 1 cn rice
- 3/4 cn (soup can) milk
- 1/8 t Salt
- 1/4 t Pepper

Direction

Mix the soups, milk and the rice, and pour into a 9"x13" baking pan.

Split the chicken breasts into 4 equal parts and place them on top of the soup mix. Season with the salt and pepper and whatever else you prefer

Bake in a 300? Oven for 2 hrs garnish as desired and serve.

Chicken & Rice Dinner

- 2 lb To 3 lb broiler/fryer chicken,
  cut up
- 1/4 c (to 1/3 cup) flour
- 2 T Oil
- 1 1/2 c Long grain rice
- 1 t Poultry seasoning
- 1 t Salt
- 1/2 t Pepper
- 1 c Milk
- 2 1/3 c Water
- Chopped fresh parsley

Direction

Dredge chicken pieces in flour. In a skillet, heat oil on medium and brown chicken on all sides. Meanwhile, combine rice, poultry seasoning, salt, pepper, milk and water. Pour into a greased 13x9x2"

baking pan. Top with chicken. Cover tightly with foil and bake at 350

degrees for 55 minutes or until rice and chicken are tender. Sprinkle with parsley before serving.

Chicken & Rice Jambalaya Style

- 2 slices of bacon

- 2 c water

- 1 package lipton cajun style rice

- 2 t ketchup

- 3/4 lb chicken breast meat

- 1/2 c frozen peas (optional)

Direction

Cut chicken into 1 inch squares. set aside. In a large skillet, cook Bacon until crisp. Remove from skillet and crumble. Set aside. Into the skillet place the water, rice & Cajun style sauce and the ketchup.

135

Bring to a boil. Reduce heat and simmer for 3 minutes, stirring occasionally. Stir in chicken and bacon (also peas if used). Cook another 5 to 10 minutes or until chicken and rice be tender. Each

Chicken and Rice

- 6 Bonless chicken breasts, skinned

- 2 cn Cream of chicken soup

- 1 cn Cream of mushroom soup

- 1 package Rice-a-roni (chicken flavor)

- 1 Salt and pepper to taste

Direction

In slow cooker put chicken breast with canned soups, alt and ppper.

Cook all day on LOW (approx. 10 hrs. or until chicken is tender). Fix Rice-A-Roni per directions on box. Put on plate and place chicken and gravy on top.

137

Printed in Great Britain
by Amazon

22946016R00077